THE MESSAGE OF FATIMA

Lucia Speaks

In accord with Canon 827 of the New Code of Canon Law, this publication has been submitted to a censor of the Diocese and nothing being found contrary to faith and morals, we hereby grant permission in accord with Canon 824 that it be published.

Rev. Msgr. John B. Szymanski,
Vicar General
Diocese of Metuchen,
November 3, 1997

N.B. The ecclesiastical permission implies nothing more than the material contained in the publication has been examined by diocesan censors and nothing contrary to faith and morals has been found therein.

THE MESSAGE OF FATIMA

Lucia Speaks

Sr. Maria Lucia
of the Immaculate Heart

Edited by John Hauf

WORLD APOSTOLATE OF FATIMA
BLUE ARMY SHRINE, U.S.A.
WASHINGTON, NEW JERSEY
www.wafusa.org   (908)689-1700

Texts excerpted from Fatima in Lucia's Own Words, edited by Fr. Louis Kondor, S.V.D. and translated from the Portuguese by the Dominican Nuns of the Perpetual Rosary, and from Jacinta, the Flower of Fatima by Fr. José Galamba de Oliveira. Translated from the Portuguese by Frs. Humberto S. Medeiros and William F. Hill. © 1982, 1972 by AMI Press.

©2007 Revised Edition

Texts compiled by Jeannette Koene & Marie Ostermann

Printed in the United States of America
All Rights Reserved

ISBN 1-56036-107-7

Editor's Note

This new and expanded edition of The Message of Fatima (popularly known as Lucia Speaks) was published on the occasion of the 80th anniversary of the Fatima apparitions and the 50th anniversary of the Blue Army of Our Lady of Fatima. It differs slightly from previous editions in that the source of the quotations by Sister Lucia, the surviving Fatima witness, is the English edition of Sister Lucia's memoirs published by the Postulation Center for the Causes of Jacinta and Francisco Marto at Fatima. The memoirs were edited by Fr. Louis Kondor, S.V.D. vice postulator for the causes of Jacinta and Francisco Marto, Blesseds at this writing. They are widely recognized as a fundamental source of information on the Fatima message.

Quotations attributed to Jacinta after the 1917 apparitions are taken from Father Oliveira's biography, Jacinta, the Flower of Fatima.

PREFACE

The news of the great happenings at Fatima in 1917 have reached the most remote corners of the earth. Yet the heavenly message which Our Lady brought to earth is still unknown to many, the message that mankind must turn from its evil ways and return to God, our Creator and Lord.

The reason for this little booklet is to make Our Lady's message known to all the world, as far as possible. This is the true message of Fatima, which very accurately reflects the Gospels, and shows the way for everyone to return to our Father's house. May this small book, with the blessings of Our Heavenly Mother, achieve its mission.

<u>WORLD APOSTOLATE OF FATIMA PRAYER CELLS</u>

WAF Prayer Cells are groups of people who gather together regularly in response to Our Lady of Fatima's requests for prayer, penance and sacrifice in reparation for sin in order to bring about the conversion of sinners necessary to save souls from hell, bring peace to the world, and protect and strengthen the Church.

There are many thousands of WAF Prayer Cell members throughout the world who are united, not only in purpose, but also in the charity they bestow upon one another as they add to their own intentions those of their brother and sister members throughout the world each time they gather to pray.

The WAF Prayer Cell is not simply one among the myriads of "prayer groups." It's a great deal more.

- The motive for participation is specifically to do what Our Lady of Fatima asked us to do.

- The intentions Our Lady of Fatima asked us to pray for are included.

- All of the prayers of the children of Fatima are included in the prayers prayed.

- A portion of each gathering is devoted to a systematic study of the Fatima apparitions, Our Lady's message of Hope to the world and our Faith.

- The training and certification of WAF Prayer Cell Leaders by a Pontifical Association gives assurance to members that everything will be authentically Catholic, in communion with the Church and in concert with the New Evangelization.

If you would like to join a WAF Prayer Cell, or if you'd like to become a WAF Prayer Cell Leader and establish one where you live, please contact:

Deacon Bob Ellis
920-371-1931
rellis@bluearmy.com
soul@bluearmy.com
www.wafusa.org

INTRODUCTION

God prepares those souls whom He has chosen to perform some extraordinary mission in the world. The more carefully He prepares them, the greater is the importance of the mission for all mankind.

This is especially true in regard to the three little shepherds of Fatima to whom Our Lady appeared, and to whom She confided a message that crosses all frontiers, and is directed to all men of good will.

First of all, God willed that they should be born into deeply Christian families, where they were brought up and educated in the love of God and the fulfillment of His Commandments. Later, He sent them a celestial messenger who, during the three successive apparitions, formed and prepared them in order to receive, from the Blessed Virgin Mary Herself, the great message of salvation so that men would come back once more to the ways of God.

Because it is of primary importance that all should know the facts, we now present them according to the account given by Sister Lucia in her memoirs. Sister was providentially left in the world to faithfully transmit to us the requests of Our Lady of the Rosary of Fatima.

The Apparitions of the Angel of Peace

In Lucia's Own Words

First Apparition of the Angel

The dates I cannot set down with certainty, because, at that time, I did not know how to reckon the years, the months, or even the days of the week. But I think it must have been in the spring of 1916 that the angel appeared to us for the first time in our Loca do Cabeço.

As I have already written in my account of Jacinta, we climbed the hillside in search of shelter. After having taken our lunch and said our prayers, we began to see, some distance off, above the trees that stretched away towards the east, a light, whiter than snow, in the form of a young man, transparent, and brighter than crystal pierced by the rays of the sun. As he drew nearer, we could distinguish his features more and more clearly. We were surprised, absorbed, and struck dumb with amazement.

On reaching us, he said

"Do not be afraid. I am the Angel of Peace. Pray with me."

Kneeling on the ground, he bowed down until his forehead touched the earth. Led by a supernatural impulse, we did the same, and repeated the words which we heard him say:

"My God, I believe, I adore, I hope and I love Thee! I beg pardon of Thee for those who do not believe, do not adore, do not hope and do not love Thee!"

Having repeated these words three times, he rose and said:

"Pray thus. The Hearts of Jesus and Mary are attentive to the voice of your supplications." Then he disappeared.

The supernatural atmosphere which enveloped us was so intense, that we were for a long time scarcely aware of our own existence, remaining in the same posture in which he had left us, and continually repeating the same prayer. The presence of God made itself felt so intimately and so intensely that we did not even venture to speak to one another. Next day, we were still immersed in this spiritual atmosphere, which only gradually began to disappear.

It did not occur to us to speak about this apparition, nor did we think of recommending that it be kept secret. The very apparition itself imposed secrecy. It was so intimate, that it was not easy to speak of it at all. The impression it made upon us was all the greater perhaps, in that it was the first such manifestation that we had experienced.

The Apparition of the Angel of Peace is depicted in this monument located in the Loca do Cabeço, the location in which the event occurred.

Second Apparition of the Angel

The second apparition must have been at the height of summer, when the heat of the day was so intense that we had to take the sheep home before noon and only let them out again in the early evening.

We went to spend the siesta hours in the shade of the trees which surrounded the well that I have already mentioned several times. Suddenly, we saw the same angel right beside us.

"What are you doing?" he asked. "Pray! Pray very much! The Hearts of Jesus and Mary have designs of mercy on you. Offer prayers and sacrifices constantly to the Most High."

"How are we to make sacrifices?" I asked.

"Make of everything you can a sacrifice, and offer it to God as an act of reparation for the sins by which He is offended, and in supplication for the conversion of sinners. You will thus draw down peace upon your country.

"I am its Angel Guardian, the Angel of Portugal. Above all, accept and bear with submission, the suffering which the Lord will send you."

These words were indelibly impressed upon our minds. They were like a light which made us understand who God is, how He loves us and desires to be loved, the value of sacrifice, how pleasing it is to Him and how, on account of it, He grants the grace of conversion to sinners.

It was for this reason that we began, from then on, to offer to the Lord all that mortified us, without, however, seeking out other forms of mortification and penance, except that we remained for hours on end with our foreheads touching the ground, repeating the prayer the angel had taught us.

Third Apparition of the Angel

It seems to me that the third apparition must have been in October, or towards the end of September, as we were no longer returning home for siesta.

As I have already written in my account of Jacinta, we went one day from Pregueira (a small olive grove belonging to my parents) to the Lapa, making our way along the slope of the hill on the side facing Aljustrel and Casa Velha. We said our Rosary there and the prayer the Angel had taught us at the first apparition.

While we were there, the angel appeared to us for the third time, holding a chalice in his hands, with a Host above it from which some drops of Blood were falling into the sacred vessel. Leaving the chalice and the Host suspended in the air, the angel prostrated himself on the ground and repeated this prayer three times:

"Most Holy Trinity, Father, Son and Holy Spirit, I adore You profoundly. I offer Thee the most precious Body, Blood, Soul and Divinity of Jesus Christ, present in all the tabernacles of the world, in reparation for the outrages, sacrileges and indifference with which He is offended by the infinite merits of the Sacred Heart, and the Immaculate Heart of Mary, I beg of Thee the conversion of poor sinners."

Then, rising, he once more took the chalice and the

Host in his hands. He gave the Host to me, and to Jacinta and Francisco he gave the Contents of the chalice to drink, saying as he did so: "Take and drink the Body and Blood of Jesus Christ, horribly outraged by ungrateful men. Repair their crimes and console your God." Once again, he prostrated himself on the ground and repeated with us three times more, the same prayer "Most Holy Trinity, . . ." and then disappeared.

Impelled by the power of the supernatural that enveloped us, we imitated all that the angel had done, prostrating ourselves on the ground as he did and repeating the prayers that he said. The force of the presence of God was so intense that it absorbed us and almost completely annihilated us. It seemed to deprive us even of the use of our bodily senses for a considerable length of time. During those days, we performed all our exterior actions as though guided by that same supernatural being who was impelling us thereto. The peace and happiness which we felt were great but wholly interior, for our souls were completely immersed in God. The physical exhaustion that came over us was also great.

I do not know why, but the apparitions of Our Lady produced in us very different effects. We felt the same intimate joy, the same peace and happiness, but instead of physical prostration, an expansive ease of movement; instead of this annihilation in the Divine Presence, a joyful exultation; instead of the difficulty speaking, we felt a certain communicative enthusiasm. Despite these feelings, however, we felt inspired to be silent, especially concerning certain things.

The Basilica of Our Lady of the Rosary of Fatima is a beacon of hope for millions of pilgrims from around the world each year.

Jacinta, Francisco and Lucia in a photograph from 1917. On May 13, 1989, Pope John Paul II venerated Jacinta and Francisco Marto, in a ceremony in Fatima.

The Apparitions
of Our Lady

First Apparition of Our Lady
May 13, 1917

High up on the slope in the Cova da Iria, I was playing with Jacinta and Francisco at building a little stone wall around a clump of furze. Suddenly we saw what seemed to be a flash of lightning.

"We'd better go home," I said to my cousins, "that's lightning; we may have a thunderstorm."

"Yes, indeed!" they answered.

We began to go down the slope, hurrying the sheep along towards the road. We were more or less half-way down the slope, and almost level with a large holmoak tree that stood there, when we saw another flash of lightning. We had only gone a few steps further when, there before us on a small holmoak, we beheld a Lady all dressed in white. She was more brilliant than a crystal glass filled with sparkling water, when the rays of the glass filled with sparkling water, when the rays of the burning sun shine through it.

We stopped, astounded, before the apparition. We were so close, just a few feet from Her, that we were bathed in the light which surrounded Her,

9

or rather, which radiated from Her. Then Our Lady spoke to us:

"Do not be afraid. I will do you no harm."

"Where are you from?"

"I am from heaven."

"What do you want of me?"

"I have come to ask you to come here for six months in succession, on the 13th day, at this same hour. Later on, I will tell you who I am and what I want. Afterwards, I will return here yet a seventh time."

"Shall I go to heaven too?"

"Yes, you will."

"And Jacinta?"

"She will go also."

"And Francisco?"

"He will go there too, but he must say many Rosaries."

Then I remembered to ask about two girls who had died recently. They were friends of mine and used to come to my home to learn weaving with my eldest sister.

"Is Maria das Neves in heaven?"

"Yes, she is."(I think she was about 16 years old).

"And Amélia?"

"She will be in purgatory until the end of the world." (It seems to me that she was between 18 and 20 years of age.)

"Are you willing to offer yourselves to God and bear all the sufferings He wills to send you, as an act of reparation for the sins by which He is offended, and of supplication for the conversion of sinners?" "Yes, we are willing."

"Then you are going to have much to suffer, but the grace of God will be your comfort."

As She pronounced these last words ". . . the grace of God will be your comfort," Our Lady opened Her hands for the first time, communicating to us a light so intense that, as it streamed from Her hands, its rays penetrated our hearts and the innermost depths of our souls, making us see ourselves in God, Who was that light, more clearly than we see ourselves in the best of mirrors. Then, moved by an interior impulse that was also communicated to us, we fell on our knees, repeating in our hearts:

"O most Holy Trinity, I adore Thee! My God, my God, I love Thee in the most Blessed Sacrament!"

After a few moments, Our Lady spoke again:

"Pray the Rosary every day, in order to obtain peace for the world, and the end of the war."

Then She began to rise serenely, going up towards the east, until She disappeared in the immensity of space. The light that surrounded Her seemed to open up a path before Her in the firmament, and for this reason we sometimes said that we saw heaven opening.

---

1. This "seventh time" refers to June 16, 1921, on the eve of Lucia's departure for Vilar de Oporto. The apparition in question was of a personal nature for Lucia. She did not consider it necessary to relate in her memoirs. (Fatima in Lucia's Own Words, ed. by Fr. Louis Kondor, S.V.D., p.187).

Thousands of pilgrims watch as the statue of Our Lady of Fatima is processed towards the Basilica of Our Lady of the Rosary in Fatima, Portugal.

Second Apparition of Our Lady

June 13, 1917

As soon as Jacinta, Francisco and I had finished praying the Rosary, with a number of other people who were present, we saw once more the flash reflecting the light which was approaching (which we called lightning). The next moment, Our Lady was there on the holmoak, exactly the same as in May.

"What do you want of me?" I asked.

"I wish you to come here on the 13th of next month, to pray the Rosary every day, and to learn to read. Later, I will tell you what I want."

I asked for the cure of a sick person.

"If he is converted, he will be cured during the year."

"I would like to ask you to take us to heaven."

"Yes. I will take Jacinta and Francisco soon. But you are to stay here some time longer.

Jesus wishes to make use of you to make me known and loved. He wants to establish in the world devotion to my Immaculate Heart."

"Am I to stay here alone?" I asked, sadly.

"No, my daughter. Are you suffering a great deal? Don't lose heart. I will never forsake you. My Immaculate Heart will be your refuge and the way that will lead you to God."

As Our Lady spoke these last words, She opened Her hands and for the second time, She communicated to us the rays of that same immense light. We saw ourselves in this light, as it were, immersed in God. Jacinta and Francisco seemed to be in that part of the light which rose towards heaven, and I in that which was poured out on the earth. In front of the palm of Our Lady's right hand was a heart encircled by thorns which pierced it. We understood that this was the Immaculate Heart of Mary, outraged by the sins of humanity, and seeking reparation.

You know now, Your Excellency, what we referred to when we said that Our Lady had revealed a secret to us in June. At the time, Our Lady did not tell us to keep it secret, but we felt moved to do so by God.

---

1. Because she was in a hurry, Lucia omitted the end of the paragraph which, in other documents, reads as follows: "I promise salvation to those who embrace it, and those souls will be loved by God like flowers placed by me to adorn His throne." (Fatima in Lucia's Own Words, ed. by Fr. Louis Kondor, S.V.D., p. 187).

Third Apparition of Our Lady

July 13, 1917

A few moments after arriving at the Cova da Iria, near the holmoak, where a large number of people were praying the Rosary, we saw the flash of light once more, and a moment later Our Lady appeared on the holmoak.

"What do you want of me?" I asked.

"I want you to come here on the 13th of next month, to continue to pray the Rosary every day in honor of Our Lady of the Rosary, in order to obtain peace for the world and the end of the war, because only She can help you."

"I would like to ask You to tell us who You are, and to work a miracle so that everybody will believe that you are appearing to us."

"Continue to come here every month. In October, I will tell You who I am and what I want, and I will perform a miracle for all to see and believe."

I then made some requests, but I cannot recall now just what they were. What I do remember is that Our Lady said it was necessary for such people to pray the Rosary in order to obtain these graces during the year. And She continued:

"Sacrifice yourselves for sinners, and say many times, especially whenever you make some sacrifice: O Jesus, it is for love of Thee, for the conversion of sinners, and in reparation for the sins committed against the Immaculate Heart of Mary."

As Our Lady spoke these last words, She opened Her hands once more, as She had done during the two previous months. The rays of light seemed to penetrate the earth, and we saw as it were a sea of fire. Plunged in this fire were demons and souls in human form, like transparent burning embers, all blackened or burnished bronze, floating about in the conflagration, now raised into the air by the flames that issued from within themselves together with great clouds of smoke, now falling back on every side like sparks in huge fires, without weight or equilibrium, amid shrieks and groans of pain and despair, which horrified us and made us tremble with fear. (It must have been this sight which caused me to cry out, as people say they heard me.)

The demons could be distinguished by their terrifying and repellent likeness to frightful and unknown animals, black and transparent like burning coals. Terrified and as if to plead for succor, we looked up at Our Lady, who said to us, so kindly and so sadly:

"You have seen hell where the souls of poor sinners go. To save them, God wishes to establish in the world devotion to my Immaculate Heart. If what I say to you is done, many souls will be saved

16

and there will be peace. The war is going to end; but if people do not cease offending God, a worse one will break out during the pontificate of Pius XI. When you see a night illumined by an unknown light, know that this is the great sign given you by God that He is about to punish the world for its crimes, by means of war, famine, and persecutions of the Church and of the Holy Father.

"To prevent this, I shall come to ask for the consecration of Russia to my Immaculate Heart, and the Communion of Reparation on the First Saturdays. If my requests are heeded, Russia will be converted, and there will be peace; if not, she will spread her errors throughout the world, causing wars and persecutions of the Church. The good will be martyred, the Holy Father will have much to suffer, various nations will be annihilated. In the end, my Immaculate Heart will triumph. The Holy Father will consecrate Russia to me, and she will be converted, and a period of peace will be granted to the world. In Portugal, the dogma of the Faith will always be preserved; etc. Do not tell this to anybody. Francisco, yes, you may tell him.

"When you pray the Rosary, say after each mystery: O my Jesus, forgive us our sins, save us

1. This was thought to be an aurora borealis on the night of January 25-26, 1938, which was unusual, and always regarded by Lucia as the God-given sign which had been promised. (Fatima in Lucia's Own Words, ed. by Fr. Louis Kondor, S.V.D., p. 187).
2. It was at this point that Our Lady revealed what has become known as the Third Secret of Fatima. The secret is discussed in the appendices.

from the fires of hell. Lead all souls to Heaven, especially those most in need of Thy mercy."

After this, there was a moment of silence, and then I asked:

"Is there anything more that you want of me."

"No, I do not want anything more of you today."

Then, as before Our Lady began to ascend towards the east, until She finally disappeared in the immense distance of the firmament.

Fourth Apparition of Our Lady

August 19, 1917

As I have already said what happened on this day, I will not delay over here, but pass on to the apparition which, in my opinion, took place on the 15th1 in the afternoon. As at that time I did not yet know how to reckon the days of the month, it could be that I am mistaken. But I still have an idea that it took place on the very day that we arrived back from Vila Nova de Ourém.

I was accompanied by Francisco and his brother John. We were with the sheep in a place called Valinhos, when we felt something supernatural approaching and enveloping us. Suspecting that Our Lady was about to appear to us, and feeling sorry lest Jacinta might miss seeing her, we asked her brother to go and call her. As he was unwilling to go, I offered him two small coins, and off he ran.

Meanwhile, Francisco and I saw the flash of light, which we called lightning. Jacinta arrived, and a moment later, we saw Our Lady on a holmoak tree.

"What do you want of me?"

"I want you to continue going to the Cova da Iria on the 13th, and to continue praying the Rosary every day. In the last month, I will perform a miracle so that all may believe."

"What do you want done with the money that the people leave in the Cova da Iria?"

"Have two litters made. One is to be carried by you and Jacinta and two other girls dressed in white; the other is to be carried by Francisco and three other boys. The money from the litters is for the "festa" [feast] of Our Lady of the Rosary, and what is left over will help towards the construction of a chapel that is to be built here."

"I would like to ask you to cure some sick persons."

"Yes, I will cure some of them during the year." Then looking very sad, Our Lady said:

"Pray, pray very much, and make sacrifices for sinners; for many souls go to hell, because there are none to sacrifice themselves and to pray for them."

And she began to ascend as usual towards the east.

---

1. Lucia mentions here and also elsewhere, that the apparition occurred at Valinhos on August 15, that is, on the day of her return from Vila Nova de Ourém. This is a mistake; the day of her return from Ourém was certainly August 15, but the apparition occurred on the following Sunday, August 19, 1917 (Fatima in Lucia's Own Words, edited by Fr. Louis Kondor, S.V.D., p. 100).

Fifth Apparition of Our Lady

September 13, 1917

As the hour approached, I set out with Jacinta and Francisco, but owing to the crowds around us we could only advance with difficulty. The roads were packed with people, and everyone wanted to see us and speak to us. There was no human respect whatsoever. Simple folk, and even ladies and gentlemen, struggled to break through the crowd that pressed around us. No sooner had they reached us than they threw themselves on their knees before us, begging us to place their petitions before Our Lady. Others who could not get close to us shouted from a distance:

"For the love of God, ask Our Lady to cure my son who is a cripple!" Yet another cried out: "And to cure mine who is blind! . . . To cure mine who is deaf! . . . To bring back my husband, my son, who has gone to war! . . . To convert a sinner! . . . To give me back my health as I have tuberculosis!"

All the afflictions of poor humanity were assembled there. Some climbed up to the tops of trees and walls to see us go by, and shouted down to us. Saying yes to some,salud, que estoy tuberculoso!"
giving a hand to others and helping them up from the dusty ground, we managed to move forward, thanks to some gentlemen who went ahead and opened a passage for us through the multitude.

Now, when I read the New Testament about

those enchanting scenes of Our Lord's passing through Palestine, I think of those which Our Lord allowed me to witness, while yet a child, on the poor roads and lanes from Aljustrel to Fatima and on to the Cova da Iria! I give thanks to God, offering Him the faith of our good Portuguese people, I think: "If these people so humbled themselves before three poor children, just because they were mercifully granted the grace to speak to the Mother of God, what would they not do if they saw Our Lord Himself in person before them?"

Well, none of this was called for here! It was a distraction of my pen, leading me away where I did not mean to go. But, never mind! It's just another useless digression. I am not tearing it out, so as not to spoil the notebook.

At last, we arrived at the Cova da Iria, and on reaching the holmoak we began to say the Rosary with the people. Shortly afterwards, we saw the flash of light, and then Our Lady appeared on the holmoak.

"Continue to pray the Rosary in order to obtain the end of the war. In October Our Lord will come, as well as Our Lady of Dolors and Our Lady of Carmel. Saint Joseph will appear with the Child Jesus to bless the world. God is pleased with your sacrifices. He does not want you to sleep with the rope on, but only wear it during the daytime."

"I was told to ask you many things, the cure of some sick people, of a deaf-mute . . ."

"Yes, I will cure some, but not others. In Oc-

22

tober I will perform a miracle so that all may believe."

Then Our Lady began to rise as usual, and disappeared.

Witnesses of the October 13, 1917, Miracle of the Sun in
Fatima, Portugal.

Sixth Apparition of Our Lady

October 13, 1917

We left home quite early, expecting that we would be delayed along the way. Masses of people thronged the roads. The rain fell in torrents. My mother, her heart torn with uncertainty as to what was going to happen, and fearing it would be the last day of my life, wanted to accompany me.

On the way, the scenes of the previous month, still more numerous and moving, were repeated. Not even the muddy roads could prevent these people from kneeling in the most humble and suppliant of attitudes. We reached the holmoak in the Cova da Iria. Once there, moved by an interior impulse, I asked the people to shut their umbrellas and say the Rosary. A little later, we saw the flash of light, and then Our Lady appeared on the holmoak.

"What do you want of me?"

"I want to tell you that a chapel is to be built here in my honor. I am the Lady of the Rosary. Continue always to pray the Rosary every day. The war is going to end, and the soldiers will soon return to their homes."

"I have many things to ask you: the cure of some sick persons, the conversion of sinners, and other things . . ."

"Some yes, but not others. They must amend their lives and ask forgiveness for their sins."

Looking very sad, Our Lady said:

"Do not offend the Lord our God any more, because He is already so much offended."

Then, opening her hands, she made them reflect on the sun, and as she ascended, the reflection of her own light continued to be projected on the sun itself.

Here, Your Excellency, is the reason why I cried out to the people to look at the sun. My aim was not to call their attention to the sun, because I was not even aware of their presence. I was moved to do so under the guidance of an interior impulse.

After Our Lady had disappeared into the immense distance of the firmament, we beheld St. Joseph with the Child Jesus and Our Lady robed in white with a blue mantle, beside the sun. St. Joseph and the Child Jesus appeared to bless the world, for they traced the Sign of the Cross with their hands. When, a little later, this apparition disappeared, I saw Our Lord and Our Lady; it seemed to me that it was Our Lady of Dolors. Our Lord appeared to bless the world in the same manner as St. Joseph had done. This apparition also vanished, and I saw Our Lady once more, this time resembling Our Lady of Carmel.

---

1. Lucia refers here to the miracle promised by Our Lady on July 13. The miracle of the sun occurred at this point in Lucia's narration. Estimates of the crowd present at Fatima ranged from 50,000 to 100,000 persons. It was seen by people within a 600 square mile area (roughly 32 by 20 miles) and described by journalist Avelino de Almeida. "Before the astonished eyes of the crowd, whose aspect was biblical as they stood bareheaded, pale with fright, eagerly searching the sky, the sun trembled, made sudden incredible movements outside all cosmic laws—the sun 'danced' according to the typical expression of the people. . . . The great majority admitted to having seen the trembling and the dancing of the sun. Others affirmed that they saw the face of the Blessed Virgin, while others swore that the sun whirled on itself like a giant catherine wheel and that it lowered itself to the earth as if to burn it with its rays. Some said they saw it change colors successively." Fatima, the Great Sign, Francis Johnston, Washington, N.J., AMI Press, 1980, pp. 58-66.

Apparitions after 1917

Jacinta Marto

Francisco Marto died at his home in Aljustrel near Fatima on April 4, 1919. His sister Jacinta died in a Lisbon hospital on February 20, 1920. This chapter about Jacinta is excerpted from the book, Jacinta, the Flower of Fatima by Father Oliveira.

"Our Lady came to see us and said that she is coming very soon for Francisco to take him up to heaven. But she asked me if I still wanted to convert more sinners. I told her that I did. She told me that I was going to a hospital, and that I was going to suffer very much there, and that I should suffer for the conversion of sinners, in reparation for the sins committed against the Immaculate Heart of Mary and for the love of Jesus. . . . "

"Our Lady wants me to go to two hospitals, but it is not to be cured; it is only to suffer more for the love of Our Lord and for sinners."

The last days of Jacinta's life were spent in intimate union with the Mother of God. Because the Lady told her before she entered the hospital that she was going to die, Jacinta objected to surgical treatment. A successful operation was performed, however, and yet Jacinta grew worse. Violent pains racked her little body. Then as if by magic, four days before she died, the pains disappeared. Jacinta explained that Our Lady had again visited her, promising that in a short time she would come for her and relieve her of all pain. From that day until the moment of her death she showed no more signs of suffering.

The Lady told her that:

- the sin which leads most people to perdition is the sin of impurity.
- that luxuries have to be put aside.
- people must not be obstinate in sin as they have been until now.
- people must perform great penances.

The Lady was very sad as She said these words. For that reason Jacinta used to say again and again, "Oh, I feel so sorry for Our Lady! I feel so sorry for her!"

Before her death, Jacinta revealed some little-known statements made by Our Lady:

"Tell everybody...that the Heart of Jesus wishes the Heart of Mary to be venerated at His side. Let them ask for peace through the Immaculate Heart of Mary, for God has given it to Her."

"War is a punishment for sin."

"Certain fashions will be introduced that will offend Our Lord very much."

"Many marriages are not good, they do not please Our Lord and are not of God."

"Priests must be pure, very pure. They should not busy themselves with anything except what concerns the Church and souls. The disobedience of priests to their superiors and to the Holy Father is very displeasing to Our Lord."

The Five First Saturday Devotion of Reparation

Dorothean convent, Pontevedra, Spain,

December 10, 1925

*(Sister Lucia is writing of herself in her memoirs in the third person.)

On December 10, 1925, the most holy Virgin appeared to her,1 and by her side, elevated on a luminous cloud, was a Child. The most holy Virgin rested her hand on her shoulder, and as she did so, she showed her a heart encircled by thorns, which she was holding in her other hand. At the same time, the Child said:

"Have compassion on the Heart of your most holy Mother, covered with thorns, with which ungrateful men pierce it at every moment, and there is no one to make an act of reparation to remove them."

Then the most holy Virgin said:

"Look, my daughter, at my Heart, surrounded with thorns with which ungrateful men pierce me at every moment by their blasphemies and ingratitude. You at least try to console me and say that I promise to assist at the hour of death, with the graces necessary for salvation, all those who, on the first Saturday of five consecutive months, shall confess, receive Holy Communion, recite five decades of the Rosary, and keep me company for fifteen minutes while meditating on the fifteen mysteries of the Rosary, with the intention of making reparation to me."

February 15, 1926

On February 15, 1926, the Infant Jesus apeared to her again. He asked her if she had already spread the devotion to his most holy Mother. She told Him of the confessor's difficulties, and said that Mother Superior was prepared to propagate it, but that the confessor had said that she, alone, could do nothing.

Jesus replied:

"It is true that your Superior alone can do nothing, but with my grace, she can do all."

She placed before Jesus the difficulty that some people had about confessing on Saturday, and asked that it might be valid to go to Confession within eight days. Jesus answered:

"Yes, and it could be longer still, provided that, when they receive Me, they are in the state of grace and have the intention of making reparation to the Immaculate Heart of Mary."

She then asked:

"My Jesus, what about those who forget to make this intention?"

Jesus replied:

"They can do so at their next Confession, taking advantage of the first opportunity to go to Confession."

On June 12, 1930, Sr. Lucia wrote to her priest confessor answering questions he had put to her, "Why should it be 5 Saturdays and not 9 or 7 in honor of the Sorrows of Our Lady?"

Sr. Lucia answered, "While staying in the chapel with Our Lord part of the night, between the 29th and 30th of this month of May 1930, and speaking to our good Lord...I felt myself being more possessed by the Divine Presence, and if I am not mistaken, the following was revealed to me:

"My daughter, the motive is simple: there are 5 ways in which people offend, and blaspheme against the Immaculate Heart of Mary:

1. The blasphemies against the Immaculate Conception,
2. Against Her Virginity,
3. Against Her Divine Maternity, refusing at the same time to accept Her as the Mother of all mankind,
4. Those who try publicly to implant in the children's hearts indifference, contempt and even hate against this Immaculate Mother,
5. Those who insult Her directly in Her sacred statues.

"Here, My daughter, is the motive why the Immaculate Heart of Mary made Me ask for this little act of reparation and due to it move My mercy to forgive those souls who had the misfortune of offending Her. As for you, try incessantly with all your prayers and sacrifices to move Me into mercifulness toward those poor souls."

Sister Lucia further answered this question, "And if one could not accomplish all those obligations on a Saturday, would Sunday not do?"

"The practice of this devotion will be equally accepted on the Sunday following the first Saturday, when, for just motives, My priests will allow it."

On May 18, 1936, Sr. Lucia wrote to Fr. Gonzalvez, having asked Our Lord why He wouldn't convert Russia without the Holy Father making the Collegial Consecration:

"Because I want my whole Church to acknowledge that consecration as a triumph of the Immaculate Heart of Mary, so that it may extend its cult later on, and put the devotion to this Immaculate Heart beside the devotion to My Sacred Heart."

Joe De Vito's rendering of the vision of the Trinity and
Our Lady as seen by Sister Lucia in the Dorothean convent at Tuy, Spain on June 13, 1929.

THE LAST VISION

Dorothean convent, Tuy, Spain, June 13, 1929

This vision was granted to Sister Lucia on June 13, 1929, in the chapel of her convent at Tuy, Spain.

It was at this time that Our Lady informed me that the moment had come in which she wished me to make known to Holy Church her desire for the Consecration of Russia, and her promise to convert it.

I had sought and obtained permission from my superiors and confessor to make a Holy Hour from eleven o'clock until midnight, every Thursday to Friday night. Being alone one night, I knelt near the altar rail in the middle of the chapel and, prostrate, I prayed the prayers of the angel. Feeling tired, I then stood up and continued to say the prayers with my arms in the form of a cross. The only light was that of the sanctuary lamp. Suddenly the whole chapel was illumined by a supernatural light, and above the altar appeared a cross of light, reaching to the ceiling. In a brighter light on the upper part of the cross, could be seen the face of a man and his body as far as the waist; upon his breast was a dove of light; nailed to the cross was the body of another man. A little below the waist, I could see a chalice and a large Host suspended in the air, on to which

36

drops of Blood were falling from the face of Jesus Crucified and from the wound in his side. These drops ran down on to the Host and fell into the chalice. Beneath the right arm of the cross was Our Lady and in her hand was her Immaculate Heart. (It was Our Lady of Fatima, with her Immaculate Heart in her left hand, without sword or roses, but with a crown of thorn and flames.) Under the left arm of the cross, large letters, as if of crystal clear water which ran down upon the altar, formed these words: "Grace and Mercy."

I understood that it was the Mystery of the Most Holy Trinity which was shown to me, and I received lights about this mystery which I am not permitted to reveal.

Our Lady then said to me: "The moment has come in which God asks the Holy Father, in union with all the bishops of the world, to make the consecration of Russiapromising to save it by this means. . . ."

Our Lady's Words

1. OFFERING: "Will you offer yourselves to God, and bear with submission all the sufferings He sends you, in reparation for the sins that offend Him, and for the conversion of sinners?"

2. BLESSED SACRAMENT: Our Lady opened her hands and flooded the children in light. They fell to their knees, repeating: "Most Holy Trinity, I adore Thee! My God, my God, I love Thee in the Most Blessed Sacrament."

3. HEAVEN: "I come down from heaven." Our Lady promised that the children to whom she appeared would go to heaven, but one of them would have to pray many Rosaries "first."

4. PURGATORY: "She is in purgatory.... " (In reference to a friend, Amelia, who had recently died.)

5. ROSARY: "Pray the Rosary every day to obtain peace for the world and the end of the war. O my Jesus, forgive us our sins, save us from the fires of hell; lead all souls to heaven, especially those most in need of Thy mercy."

6. IMMACULATE HEART: "My Immaculate Heart will be your refuge and the way that will lead you to God."

7. SACRIFICES: "Make sacrifices for sinners, and say often, especially while making a sacrifice: 'O Jesus, this is for love of Thee. for the conver-

38

sion of sinners and in reparation for sins committed against the Immaculate Heart of Mary."

8. HELL: "You have seen hell, where the souls of poor sinners go. It is to save them that God wants to establish in the world devotion to my Immaculate Heart. If you do what I tell you, many souls will be saved, and there will be peace." Before Our Lady spoke these words, she opened her hands, as Lucia says in her Memoirs, and "we saw a sea of fire Plunged in this flame were devils and souls that looked like transparent embers; others were black or bronze, and in human form; these were suspended in flames.... "

9. FIVE WARNINGS: "If my requests are not heeded, Russia will spread her errors throughout the world, provoking wars and persecutions of the Church; the good will be martyred, the Holy Father will have much to suffer, and various entire nations will be annihilated."

10. PEACE: "If my requests are fulfilled, Russia will be converted and there will be peace.... Finally, my Immaculate Heart will triumph. . . an era of peace will be granted to mankind."**11. PRAYER:** "Pray, pray a great deal and make sacrifices for sinners, for many souls go to hell because they have no one to pray and make sacrifices for them."

12. AMENDMENT OF LIFE: "I have come to ask the faithful to amend their lives and ask pardon for their sins. They must cease offending

39

God, who is already too much offended!"

13. ST. JOSEPH: The only saint who appears at Fatima besides Our Lady. St. Joseph held the Child Jesus in his arms and blessed the people.

14. SCAPULAR OF MOUNT CARMEL: In the final vision, on October 13, 1917, Our Lady appeared in the Carmelite habit wearing the Brown Scapular, highlighting the importance of this sacramental.

15. FIRST SATURDAY DEVOTION: "I promise to assist at the hour of death, with all the graces necessary for salvation, to all who on the first Saturday of five consecutive months: (1) Confess, (2) Receive Holy Communion, (3) Pray five decades of the Rosary, and (4) Keep me company for fifteen minutes while meditating on the mysteries of the Rosary, all with the intention of making reparation to my Immaculate Heart."

"Our Lady also said that we should pray much and that we should make many sacrifices of the senses, which please Our Lord so much; that we should love God with our whole heart; that we should respect priests, who are the salt of the earth and serve to direct souls onto the path to Heaven..."

The Rich Content of the Message of Fatima

The message of Fatima which springs from the apparitions of Our Lady, is a solid blueprint for life. It cries out to be put into practice for the good of the world, and the salvation of souls. Its teachings are in harmony with the Gospel, calling to mind the following elements with new emphasis

- The mystery of the Blessed Trinity;
- The providence of God, which directs and governs the world and presides over the events of human history;
- The omnipotence and omniscience of God, Who knows and realizes all things according to his exalted designs. It foretold future events and revealed miraculous signs to prove the truth of God's predictions;
- God, Who rewards or punishes, according to the good or evil done, though He is ever merciful towards sinners;
- The reality of heaven, hell and purgatory;
- The existence of Guardian Angels, not only of individuals but also of nations;

- The real presence of Christ in the Most Blessed Sacrament, and the necessity and value of Holy Communion;
- Sanctity as a condition of true happiness even on earth, and docility and correspondence to grace, the mysterious mixture of divine action and human effort;
- The reality of sin as an offense against God with its tragic consequences for sinners and nations;
- The flight from sin and amendment of life as an indispensable condition of the state of grace;
- The Christian solidarity of the Mystical Body of Christ;
- The intercession of the Mother of God as a powerful mediatrix and dispenser of grace;
- The necessity of penance and prayer, with their value of atonement and intercession;
- The love of the Heart of Jesus and of the Immaculate Heart of Mary—the great revelation of Fatima;
- The importance of Marian devotions, particularly, the excellence and efficacy of the Rosary, the new devotion of the first Saturdays, and

the value of Consecration of the
Immaculate Heart of Mary;

- The powerful action of grace, which
  so transformed the three little children
  at Fatima and led them to such a close
  union with God.
- Russia, simultaneously a scourge that
  punishes the sins of the world, and
  the object of Divine Mercy, by the
  promise of its conversion through the
  intermediary of the Heart of Mary;
- The sanctification of the family, in imi
  tation of the vivid scene of the last
  apparition;
- Devotion to the Holy Father and the
  necessity of purity and modesty;
- The final triumph of the
  Immaculate Heart of Mary.

Pope John Paul's first encounter with Sr. Lucia took place exactly one year after the attempt on his life in St. Peter's Square in 1981. On that occasion he ordered the bullet that was found in the jeep in which he was riding, be set in the crown of the image of the Virgin of Fatima in gratitude to her for saving his life, as the Third Secret revealed.

Appendix I

The Third Secret of Fatima

Translation of the Original Text written by Sr. Lucia in 1944 to Bishop Leiria

J. M. J

The third part of the secret revealed at the Cova da Iria-Fatima, on 13 July 1917.

I write in obedience to you, my God, who command me to do so through his Excellency the Bishop of Leiria and through your Most Holy Mother and mine.

After the two parts which I have already explained, at the left of Our Lady and a little above, we saw an Angel with a flaming sword in his left hand; flashing, it gave out flames that looked as though they would set the world on fire; but they died out in contact with the splendour that Our Lady radiated towards him from her right hand: pointing to the earth with his right hand, the Angel cried out in a loud voice: 'Penance, Penance, Penance!'. And we saw in an immense light that is God: 'something similar to how people appear in a mirror when they pass in front of it' a Bishop dressed in White 'we had the impression that it was the Holy Father'.

Other Bishops, Priests, men and women Religious going up a steep mountain, at the top of which there was a big Cross of rough-hewn trunks as of a cork-tree with the bark; before reaching there the Holy Father passed through a big city half in ruins and half trembling with halting step, afflicted with pain and sorrow, he prayed for the souls of the corpses he met on his way; having reached the top of the mountain, on his knees at the foot of the big Cross he was killed by a group of soldiers who fired bullets and arrows at him, and in the same way there died one after another the other bishops, priests, men and women religious, and various lay people of different ranks and positions. Beneath the two arms of the cross there were two angels each with a crystal aspersorium in his hand, in which they gathered up the blood of the Martyrs and with it sprinkled the souls that were making their way to God.

Tuy-3-1-1944

Appendix II

The Third Secret of Fatima

Translation of the Pope John Paul II's Official Response to the Text of the Third Secret

To the Reverend Sister Maria Lucia of the Convent of Coimbra

In the great joy of Easter, I greet you with the words the Risen Jesus spoke to the disciples: "Peace be with you"!

I will be happy to be able to meet you on the long-awaited day of the Beatification of Francisco and Jacinta, which, please God, I will celebrate on 13 May of this year.

Since on that day there will be time only for a brief greeting and not a conversation, I am sending His Excellency Archbishop Tarcisio Bertone, Secretary of the Congregation for the Doctrine of the Faith, to speak with you. This is the Congregation which works most closely with the Pope in defending the true Catholic faith, and which since 1957, as you know, has kept your hand-written letter containing the third part of the "secret" revealed on 13 July 1917 at Cova da Iria, Fatima.

Archbishop Bertone, accompanied by the Bishop of Leiria, His Excellency Bishop Serafim de Sousa Ferreira e Silva, will come in my name to ask certain questions about the interpretation of "the third part of the secret".

Sister Maria Lucia, you may speak openly and candidly to Archbishop Bertone, who will report your answers directly to me.

I pray fervently to the Mother of the Risen Lord for you, Reverend Sister, for the Community of Coimbra and for the whole Church. May Mary, Mother of pilgrim humanity, keep us always united to Jesus, her beloved Son and our brother, the Lord of life and glory.

With my special Apostolic Blessing.

IOANNES PAULUS PP. II

From the Vatican, 19 April 2000.

Pledge of Our Lady of Fatima

Dear Queen and Mother, who promised at Fatima to convert Russia and bring peace to all mankind, in reparation for my sins and the sins of the whole world, I solemnly promise to your Immaculate Heart:

1. To offer up every day the sacrifices demanded by my daily duty.
2. To pray part of the Rosary* daily while meditating on the Mysteries.
3. To wear the Scapular of Mount Carmel as profession of this promise and as an act of consecration to you.
4. To accomplish the devotion of the Five First Saturdays of the month, including fifteen minutes of meditation on the Mysteries of the Rosary.

I shall renew this promise often, especially in moments of temptation.

*Usually understood to mean at least five decades.

Note: This pledge is not a vow and does not bind under sin. Nevertheless, it is a promise of love; your word to your heavenly Mother.

Morning Offering

O my God, in union with the Immaculate Heart of Mary (here kiss your Brown Scapular as a sign of your consecration—this carries a partial indulgence), I offer Thee the Precious Blood of Jesus from all the altars throughout the world, joining with It the offering of my every thought, word and action of this day.

O my Jesus, I desire today to gain every indulgence and merit I can, and I offer them, together with myself, to Mary Immaculate—that she may best apply them to the interests of thy most Sacred Heart. Precious Blood of Jesus, save us! Immaculate Heart of Mary, pray for us! Sacred Heart of Jesus, have mercy on us!

SUBSCRIBE
TO
Soul

Now that you know the Message of Fatima, why not make a difference in the world?

Join the World Apostolate of Fatima

Pope John Paul II has said that the Fatima message is more relevant today than ever (Fatima, May 13, 1982) and that it can be synthesized in Christ's own words: "The kingdom of God is at hand. Repent, and believe in the Gospel" (Vatican City, May 15, 1991)

Write: The Blue Army, Box 976, Washington, NJ 07882

Toll Free: (866) 513-1917 **Web:** www.wafusa.org

I wish to further the work of Our Lady of Fatima through the Blue Army.

Name _____

Address _____

City _____

State _____ Zip _____

☐ Please send me the World Apostolate of Fatima Pledge and information about the Apostolate.

☐ Accept my donation of $ _____ to further the work of the World Apostolate of Fatima.

☐ Please send me information on how to honor Our Lady in my Will

---

Fatima Prayer Cell Program

The World Apostolate of Fatima, USA
Washington, New Jersey
www.wafusa.org.
(908) 689-1700, ext. 18

©1996, 2008 World Apostolate of Fatima, USA/Blue Army, USA

Photos:
©World Apostolate of Fatima, USA/Blue Army, USA

Scripture References from:
The Holy Bible, Douay-Rheims Version
©2000 Tan Books and Publishers, Inc

Quotations contained in this booklet pertaining to the Apparitions and Miracle of Fatima: Fatima in Lucia's Own Words, Edited by Fr. Louis Kondor, S.V.D.

Icon artwork courtesy of Deacon Charles Rohrbacher

ISBN 1-56036-083-6

Table of Contents

CONTENTS

v

WORLD APOSTOLATE OF FATIMA PRAYER CELLS

WAF Prayer Cells are groups of people who gather together regularly in response to Our Lady of Fatima's requests for prayer, penance and sacrifice in reparation for sin in order to bring about the conversion of sinners necessary to save souls from hell, bring peace to the world, and protect and strengthen the Church.

There are many thousands of WAF Prayer Cell members throughout the world who are united, not only in purpose, but also in the charity they bestow upon one another as they add to their own intentions those of their brother and sister members throughout the world each time they gather to pray.

The WAF Prayer Cell is not simply one among the myriads of "prayer groups." It's a great deal more.

- The motive for participation is specifically to do what Our Lady of Fatima asked us to do.

- The intentions Our Lady of Fatima asked us to pray for are included.

- All of the prayers of the children of Fatima are included in the prayers prayed.

- A portion of each gathering is devoted to a systematic study of the Fatima apparitions, Our Lady's message of Hope to the world and our Faith.

- The training and certification of WAF Prayer Cell Leaders by a Pontifical Association gives assurance to members that everything will be authentically Catholic, in communion with the Church and in concert with the New Evangelization.

If you would like to join a WAF Prayer Cell, or if you'd like to become a WAF Prayer Cell Leader and establish one where you live, please contact:

Deacon Bob Ellis
920-371-1931
rellis@bluearmy.com
soul@bluearmy.com
www.wafusa.org

Introduction

The Fatima Prayer Cell of Holiness is a weekly or monthly spiritual gathering for small group prayer before the Blessed Sacrament or in a home. Members endeavor to grow in holiness by responding to Our Lady's requests for prayer, penance and sacrifice in a spirit of reparation to the Sacred Heart of Jesus and the Immaculate Heart of Mary and for the conversion of poor sinners. Thereby they work to bring about the triumph of the Immaculate Heart and promised era of peace to mankind.

It may be said that the Prayer Cell began in 1916 with the appearance of the Angel of Peace to the three shepherd children, Lucia, Francisco and Jacinta. In 1917, Our Lady appeared and told them to pray and make sacrifices for sinners. The children discussed the meaning of the message given by the Angel and Our Lady. The shepherd children encouraged each other to pray and make sacrifices. Prayer cell members do the same.

Why is it called a "Cell"? Just as cells form the human body by dividing and growing, a Prayer Cell should do the same after there are 8-10 members, or if they have completed a level within the Formation Program. The group then splits and forms a new Prayer Cell. This is how the Prayer Cell grows, multiplies and spreads the holiness of Fatima within the Church, and fills people with the prayerful spirit of Our Lady's Message.

There is nothing difficult in starting the Prayer

Cell Program. You can start a Prayer Cell in your parish with only two or more people. Simply get together with your family, several of your friends or fellow parishioners. Contact your pastor for permission to meet in the church on a day and time decided beforehand by the consensus of the group. Follow the prayer program as contained in this booklet. If for some reason you cannot obtain permission to meet in a church, begin a Prayer Cell in your home.

This booklet presents a simple format for use by members of the Prayer Cell Program. Other materials for spiritual reading are also listed towards the end of this booklet for additional study. It is highly recommended that the Prayer Cell Formation Program (see page 53) be used in conjunction with this booklet for an in-depth study of the Fatima Message and to help your Cell grow and divide into two, three and four cells as you advance through the formation process.

May God bless you in your love for Our Lady and your desire to grow in holiness for the glory of God and the salvation of souls. By learning, living and spreading Our Lady's Message, you do your part to help bring us another step closer to the promised triumph of the Immaculate Heart of Mary.

Qualification: In this booklet you will notice that Our Lady's pronouns are capitalized. This is to bring to mind the Divine prerogatives which Our Lord has been pleased to grant Her due to His magnanimous generosity.

Suggestions for Keeping the Rosary "Fresh"

Quotes excerpted from Rosarium Virginis Mariae by Pope John Paul II

LEADER'S INSTRUCTIONS:

It is recommended that Prayer Cell members read Pope John Paul II's apostolic letter Rosarium Virginis Mariae, which can be downloaded from the Vatican's website, http://www.vatican.va. Listed below are some recommended practices and considerations given by the Holy Father in the recitation of the Rosary. Each Prayer Cell is encouraged to vary the way the Rosary is recited from time to time by using one or more of his many suggestions so as to keep the recitation "fresh" as a method of contemplation.

SCRIPTURE READING [#30]:

"As we listen, we are certain that this is the Word of God, spoken for today and spoken 'for me...' It is not a matter of recalling information but of allowing God to speak."

Read a Bible passage. The leader is free to choose either the one in the booklet, part of which is contained in the passage marked

"+", or one of the other passages listed. Passages in this booklet are quoted from the Douay-Rheims Version of the Bible except for the Fifth Glorious Mystery, which is taken from the Office of Readings. However, any approved version of the Bible may be used.

USE OF ICONS [#29]:

"Announcing each mystery, and perhaps even using a suitable icon to portray it, is as it were to open up a scenario on which to focus our attention."

MEDITATIONS [#30]:

"In certain solemn communal celebrations, this word can be appropriately illustrated by a brief commentary."

Two brief commentaries are offered:
■ *A Scripture meditation and*
■ *A Fatima reflection.*
These are optional. One or both may be used.

SILENCE [#31]:

"After the announcement of the mystery and the proclamation of the word, it is fitting to pause and focus one's attention for a suitable period of time on the mystery concerned, before moving into vocal prayer."

THE "OUR FATHER" [#32]:

"...it is natural for the mind to be lifted up towards the Father. In each of his mysteries, Jesus always leads us to the Father..

THE TEN HAIL MARYS [#33]:

"These words express...the wonder of heaven and earth; they...give us a glimpse of God's own wonderment as he contemplates his 'masterpiece'...The repetition of the Hail Mary in the Rosary gives us a share in God's own wonder and pleasure..."

THE NAME OF JESUS [#33]:

"...it is precisely the emphasis given to the name of Jesus and to his mystery that is the sign of a meaningful and fruitful recitation of the Rosary. Pope Paul VI drew attention ...to the custom in certain regions of highlighting the name of Christ by the addition of a clause referring to the mystery being contemplated."

Particular emphasis should be given to the Holy Name of Jesus - a bowing of the head or an optional clause may be added with each Hail Mary after reciting His Name, e.g. "Jesus Incarnate." A clause is offered in quotes under the name of the Mystery and is taken from The Secret of the

Rosary by St. Louis de Montfort (except for the Luminous Mysteries).

CONTEMPLATION [#11]:

"Mary constantly sets before the faithful the 'mysteries' of her Son, with the desire that the contemplation of those mysteries will release all their saving power. In the recitation of the Rosary, the Christian community enters into contact with the memories and the contemplative gaze of Mary."

GLORY BE [#34]:

"It is important that the Gloria, the high-point of contemplation, be given due prominence in the Rosary. In public recitation it could be sung..."

FRUITS OF THE MYSTERY [#35]:

"...it is worthwhile to note that the contemplation of the mysteries could better express their full spiritual fruitfulness if an effort were made to conclude each mystery with a prayer for the fruits specific to that particular mystery."

Program for Prayer Cell of Holiness

Please Stand

Fatima Ave:

Refrain: Ave, Ave, Ave Maria.
                   Ave, Ave, Ave Maria.

1   In Fatima's cova
                   On the 13th of May
                   The Virgin Maria
                   Appeared at midday.

Refrain

2   To three shepherd children
                   The Virgin then spoke
                   A message so hopeful
                   With peace for all folk.

Refrain

3   With sweet Mother's pleading
                   She asked us to pray.
                   Do penance, be modest,
                   The Rosary each day.

Refrain

Sacrifice Prayer:

All of our actions should begin with this prayer. "Make everything you can a sacrifice..." the Angel told us at Fatima.

"O my Jesus, it is for love of You, for the conversion of sinners, and in reparation for the sins committed against the Immaculate Heart of Mary."

Mission Statement:

In order to establish devotion to Mary's Immaculate Heart in the world, and to place this devotion alongside devotion to the Most Sacred Heart of Jesus, we desire to live and spread Our Lady's Fatima Message, cease offending God, pray and make reparation for sin. By signing the Pledge of Our Lady of Fatima, and trusting in Mary's intercession, we hope to obtain the salvation of souls, the triumph of Mary's Immaculate Heart, and an era of peace for all mankind.

Pledge of Our Lady of Fatima:

Dear Queen and Mother, who promised at Fatima to convert Russia and bring peace to all mankind, in reparation for my sins and the sins of the whole world, I solemnly promise to your Immaculate Heart:

1. To offer up every day the sacrifices demanded by my daily duty.

2. To pray part of the Rosary daily while meditating on the Mysteries.

3. To wear the Scapular of Mount Carmel as profession of this promise and as an act of consecration to you.

4. To accomplish the devotion of the Five First Saturdays of the month, including fifteen minutes of meditation on the Mysteries of the Rosary.

I shall renew this promise often, especially in moments of temptation.

Please kneel

PRAYERS FROM FATIMA:

These next two prayers were taught by the Angel while prostrate and should be said often in reparation. Prostration is encouraged when possible.

PARDON PRAYER

"My God, I believe, I adore, I hope, and I love You! I beg pardon for those who do not believe, do not adore, do not hope, and do not love You."

(3x)

ANGEL'S PRAYER:

"Most Holy Trinity, Father, Son and Holy Spirit, I adore You profoundly, and I offer You the most precious Body, Blood, Soul, and Divinity of Jesus Christ, present in all the tabernacles of the world, in reparation for the outrages, sacrileges and indifference with which He Himself is offended. By the infinte merits of the Sacred Heart of Jesus and the

Immaculate Heart of Mary, I beg the conversion of poor sinners.

Eucharistic Prayer

"O most Holy Trinity, I adore You! My God, my God, I love You in the most Blessed Sacrament!"

World Apostolate of Fatima Universal Prayer Cell Intentions

Leader: Gathered together in a heartfelt spirit of prayer, penance and reparation for sin in response to the urgent requests of Our Lady of Fatima, and united in fraternal affection and purpose with all members of World Apostolate of Fatima Prayer Cells throughout the world, we pray for the following intentions:

Leader: For the salvation of souls - for our own souls; for those of our families and friends; for those of all members of the World Apostolate of Fatima; and especially for those of poor sinners who have no one to make reparation for their sins or pray for their conversion, we pray.
Response: O Lord, save us all.

Leader: For world peace: that as people turn away from sin and back to God peace may come to them, to their families, to their nations and to the world, we pray.
Response: O Lord, bring us peace.

LEADER: For the guidance and protection of Holy Mother Church - the bark of Peter - as she sails upon the stormy seas caused by sin and corruption in the world striving to fulfill her sacred mission as the instrument of the grace of salvation for all, we pray..

RESPONSE: O Lord, guide and protect your Church.

LEADER: For the guidance, protection and consolation of the Pope as he courageously mans the helm of Peter's Bark, and for all those united with him in carrying out the mission of the Church, we pray.

RESPONSE: O Lord, guide, protect, and console them.

LEADER: For those suffering from all manner of physical, emotional or other ailment, that they may recognize the redemptive value of their suffering; offer it in reparation for sin; and, God willing, be restored to good health, we pray.

RESPONSE: O Lord, console them and heal them.

LEADER: For all members of the World Apostolate of Fatima, that they remain faithful in honoring Our Lady's requests and steadfast in their commitment to spreading her message, we pray.

RESPONSE: O Lord, keep us faithful and strengthen our resolve.

LEADER: For all victims of the consequences of sin - for the suffering souls in purgatory; for those enduring the plagues of war; for those suffering from the greed and injustice of others; for those mired

in lives of sexual deviancy and drug and alcohol addiction and their loved ones adversely affected; and for those holy innocents living in the wombs of mothers contemplating abortion, we pray.

RESPONSE: O Lord, send your angels to guide, protect, and console us.

LEADER: For the triumph of the Immaculate Heart of Mary; that soon there will be sufficient numbers of souls drawn away from sin and into her Immaculate Heart and the Heart of her Son so that the souls of many will be saved and the era of peace she promised to the world will at last come to fruition, we pray.

RESPONSE: O Lord, grant us the grace of devotion to the Immaculate Heart of your Mother and to your own Sacred Heart.

LEADER: For those suffering from all manner of physical, emotional or other ailment, that they may recognize the redemptive value of their suffering; offer it in reparation for sin; and, God willing, be restored to good health, we pray.

RESPONSE: O Lord, console them and heal them.

LEADER: Please add your personal intentions at this time.

[Allow time for all who wish to state their petitions.]

LEADER: Lord, we now add to these intentions the intentions of all members of World Apostolate of Fatima Prayer Cells throughout the world and ask that they be granted, for this we pray.

RESPONSE: O Lord, hear us and grant our petitions.

LEADER: For these and for all the intentions of the Sacred heart of Jesus and the Immaculate Heart of Mary and in reparation for the sins committed against them, we pray.

RESPONSE: O Lord, bring conversion to sinners and peace to the world.

LEADER: Father, we ask for all of these favors through the intercession of Our Lady of Fatima, and in the name of Jesus Christ, Your Son, who lives and reigns with you and the Holy Spirit, one God, forever and ever.

RESPONSE: *Amen.*

The Holy Rosary
With Meditations

Alternate Joyful, Luminous, Sorrowful and Glorious Mysteries for each meeting.

Begin the Rosary with the Sign of the Cross. Recite the Apostles Creed, one Our Father, three Hail Marys for the virtues of Faith, Hope, and Charity, and a Glory Be. Announce the Mystery. Recite five decades of the Rosary, meditating on the Mystery to be prayed.

Decade Prayer::
After each Mystery, recite the Decade Prayer:

Oh my Jesus, forgive us, save us from the fire of hell. Lead all souls to heaven, especially those who are most in need.

Optional Ave:
Refrain from the Fatima Ave.
May be sung after the Decade Prayer.

Refrain: Ave, Ave, Ave Maria.
Ave, Ave, Ave Maria.

The Annunciation
"Jesus Incarnate"
+Luke 1:26-38

Prayer

We offer Thee, O Lord Jesus, this decade in honor of Thy Incarnation, and we ask of Thee, through this mystery and through the intercession of Thy most Holy Mother, a profound humility.

Scripture

"...the angel Gabriel was sent from God... to a virgin espoused to a man whose name was Joseph, of the house of David; and the virgin's name was Mary. And the angel ...said unto her: 'Hail, full of grace, the Lord is with thee: blessed art thou among women...Behold thou shalt conceive in thy womb, and shalt bring forth a son; and thou shalt call his name Jesus' ... And Mary said: 'Behold the handmaid of the Lord; be it done to me according to thy word.'"

Meditation

The love of God descended upon all of humanity when the power of the Most High came upon Mary. It is in Mary that the Word was made Flesh, and it is in Mary that we receive the graces with which He wishes to visit us. Let us, within the Heart of Mary, open our hearts to receive in faith the love He wishes to pour into our souls.

Fatima Reflection

"What do you want of me?" It is to a heart thus disposed that God sends His tidings of peace, first through the Heart of Mary, and again to us, through the message given to Lucia. We are all called to give our heart to God in asking Him, "What do you want of me?" Let Him enter in.

One Our Father, 10 Hail Marys, One Glory Be, Decade Prayer

Prayer

Grace of the mystery of the Incarnation, come down into my soul and make it truly humble.

The Visitation
"Jesus Sanctifying"
+Luke 1:39-56

Prayer

We offer Thee, O Lord Jesus, this decade in honor of the Visitation of Thy Holy Mother to Her cousin St. Elizabeth, and we ask of Thee, through this mystery and through Mary's intercession, a perfect charity towards our neighbor.

Scripture

"[Mary] entered into the house of Zachary, and saluted Elizabeth...[who] cried out with a loud voice, and said: 'Blessed art thou among women, and blessed is the fruit of thy womb'... And Mary said: 'My soul doth magnify the Lord. And my spirit hath rejoiced in God my Saviour. Because He hath regarded the humility of his handmaid; ...all generations shall call me blessed...holy is his name.'"

Meditation

Mary's faith brought to us our Savior. Her visit to Elizabeth is the sharing of Her Gift of God's Promise, Whom He entrusted to Her. Our Lady's Magnificat is Her Heart's proclamation of God's goodness for those who trust that the Word of the Lord to them will be fulfilled. Let us always proclaim the greatness of the Lord! And our spirit will rejoice in God our Savior!

Fatima Reflection

The angel comes to visit Mary, God's humble handmaid in Nazareth. At Fatima, Our Lady visits poor shepherd children, just as She visited Her cousin Elizabeth. Jesus is with Mary and in Mary. In Her the splendor of God is revealed: Rays shine forth from beside Him where His power is concealed. (Malachi 3:4) Let us approach the Throne of Grace (Mary), as the children did, to ponder the words that proceed from Her lips to bring tidings of hope and peace.

One Our Father, 10 Hail Marys, One Glory Be, Decade Prayer

Prayer

Grace of the mystery of the Incarnation, come down into my soul and make it truly humble.

17

The Birth of Jesus

"Jesus Born in Poverty"

+Luke 2:1-14

Prayer

We offer Thee, O Child Jesus, this decade in honor of Thy Blessed Nativity, and we ask of Thee, through this mystery and through the intercession of Thy Blessed Mother, detachment from things of this world, love of poverty and love of the poor.

Scripture

"[Joseph] went up...to the city of David, which is called Bethlehem...to be enrolled with Mary...who was with child...And she brought forth her firstborn son, and wrapped him up in swaddling clothes, and laid him in a manger; because there was no room for them in the inn...Glory to God in the highest; and on earth peace to men of good will."

Meditation

In fulfilling the duties of their state in life, Mary and Joseph obey Caesar's decree, bearing patiently with the sufferings and inconveniences this journey entailed. Out of this silent suffering was born our Lord, Who came to be with us, and to accompany us through our own daily trials and sufferings, with a promise of peace.

Fatima Reflection

"Glory to God in the highest and on earth peace among men with whom He is pleased!" What does Our Lady say to those souls who seek peace by embracing the devotion to Her Immaculate Heart, which God willed to be made known at Fatima? *"I promise salvation"*, She says, *"and these souls will be loved by God like flowers placed by me to adorn His throne."* Jesus is born again in the hearts of those who love Him and seek to please Our Lady for His sake.

One Our Father, 10 Hail Marys, One Glory Be, Decade Prayer

Prayer

Grace of the mystery of the Nativity, come down into my soul and make me truly poor in spirit.

The Presentation of Jesus in the Temple

"Jesus Sacrificed"

+Luke 2:22-35

Prayer

We offer Thee, O Lord Jesus, this decade in honor of Thy Presentation in the Temple by the hands of Mary, and we ask of Thee, through this mystery and through the intercession of Thy Blessed Mother, the gift of wisdom and purity of heart and body.

Scripture

"...they carried him to Jerusalem, to present him to the Lord:...And to offer a sacrifice....And behold there was a man in Jerusalem named Simeon...told by God that he should not see death, before he had seen the Christ of the Lord... 'Behold this child is set for the fall, and for the resurrection of many in Israel, and for a sign which shall be contradicted; And thy own soul a sword shall pierce, that, out of many hearts, thoughts may be revealed.'"

Meditation

Mary and Joseph presented Jesus in the Temple according to the prescriptions of the law. Marvel with them at Simeon's revelations of what Jesus would accomplish during His life — a glory and tragedy to be fulfilled, both then and today: a light to those who are separated from Him, and the glory of His people, the New Israel; yet also a sign of contradiction through divisions found among us — the same sword which pierces the soul of Mary today.

Fatima Reflection

Our Lady reveals Her Heart encircled with sharp thorns on every side, outraged by the sins of humanity, and She seeks reparation. *"...God wishes to establish in the world devotion to my Immaculate Heart." "Do not offend the Lord our God anymore because He is already so much offended."*

One Our Father, 10 Hail Marys, One Glory Be, Decade Prayer

Prayer

Grace of the mystery of the Purification, come down into my soul and make it truly wise and pure.

The Finding of the Child Jesus in the Temple

"Jesus, Wisdom Manifested"

+Lucas 2: 42-52

Prayer

We offer Thee, O Lord Jesus, this decade in honor of Thy Finding in the Temple among the learned men by Our Lady, after She had lost Thee, and we ask of Thee, through this mystery and through the intercession of Thy Blessed Mother, to convert us and help us amend our lives, and also to convert all sinners, those who have fallen away from the Church, and those who do not believe in God.

Scripture

"And when he was twelve years old, they going up into Jerusalem, according to the custom of the feast, and having fulfilled the days, when they returned, the child Jesus remained in Jerusalem; and his parents knew it not... 'Son, why hast thou done so to us? behold thy father and I sought thee sorrowing'... 'How is it that you sought me? did you not know, that I must be about my father's business?'"

Meditation

Seeking Him, Mary and Joseph find Jesus on the third day. Two days of sorrow, followed by the third day of joy, turns into amazement upon their finding Him. A similar loss and finding was to come later - an event which Mary would forever ponder in Her Heart: Jesus' Death and Ressurection. This loss is one that we should never forget, lest we lose Him forever.

Fatima Reflection

Our Lady comes to a world that has largely lost Christ due to sin. Mary comes seeking Him among us, His members, to teach us how to find Him through prayer and repentance. Let us seek the Holy Face of Christ in the Eucharist - where He is really and truly present, and in each other - where He is veiled under human form, so that in loving God for Himself, and loving each other for His sake, we may experience the joy of finding Him in this life and in the next. Let us show Him to a lost and suffering world.

One Our Father, 10 Hail Marys, One Glory Be, Decade Prayer

Prayer

Grace of the mystery of the Finding of the Child Jesus in the Temple, come down into my soul and truly convert me.

The Baptism of Jesus

"Jesus Baptized"
+Mark 1:2-11,
Matthew 3:1-17 / Luke 3:15-22 / John 1:29-37

Prayer

We offer Thee, O Lord Jesus, this decade in honor of Thy Holy Baptism, and we ask of Thee, through this mystery and through the intercession of Thy Blessed Mother, a firm determination to fulfill our baptismal vows.

Scripture

"It came to pass, in those days, Jesus came from Nazareth of Galilee, and was baptized by John in the Jordan. And forthwith coming up out of the water, he saw the heavens opened, and the Spirit as a dove descending, and remaining on him. And there came a voice from heaven: 'Thou art my beloved Son; in thee I am well pleased.'"

Meditation

As the Lord Jesus submits to John's baptism of repentance and enters the waters of the Jordan River, He not only makes known His willingness to take on our sins as the Lamb of God, but He also sanctifies the waters of our own baptism. We enter into these hallowed waters, are cleansed of all sin and are drawn into the bosom of the Holy Trinity. May we have the faith to see the heaven that was torn open for us and for our salvation.

Fatima Reflection

Jesus comes to communicate His desire to form a binding Covenant of Love with the whole human race. It is already accomplished in the bond He has formed Heart to Heart with Mary – Our Two-in-One Paragon of Love and Love's response. As we have entered the waters of this Covenant at Baptism, let us now enter upon the way Jesus and Mary lived and pointed out to us in the relationship of these Two Hearts revealed in Our Lady's Message at Fatima.

One Our Father, 10 Hail Marys, One Glory Be, Decade Prayer

Prayer

Grace of the mystery of Our Lord's Baptism, come down into my soul and make me truly committed to keep my baptismal vows.

The Wedding Feast at Cana
"Jesus Manifests His Divinity"
+ John 2:1-11

Prayer

We offer Thee, O Lord Jesus, this decade in honor of the Wedding Feast at Cana where Thou didst perform Thy first miracle at the request of Thy Blessed Mother, and we ask of Thee, through this mystery and through Her intercession, the grace of fidelity and generosity in Thy service.

Scripture

"... there was a marriage in Cana of Galilee: and the mother of Jesus was there. And Jesus also was invited, and his disciples...And the wine failing, the mother of Jesus saith to him: 'They have no wine.' ... His mother saith to the waiters: 'Whatsoever he shall say to you, do ye.'"

Meditation

In order to make known to His disciples the New Covenant that will transform the old, Jesus, at the prompting of His Mother, changed water into choice wine. He performs the miracle that anticipates the transformation of wine into Blood in the Passover cup. May we find, in the faith-filled petitions of the Mother of God, a source of new faith; and may we be faithful to the sacramental grace that flows from the open side of the Lamb who was slain.

Fatima Reflection

At the Last Vision, the Eucharistic Cup receives the Blood that flows from Jesus' Face and Side, with Our Lady at His side as though to beckon us to participation: "Make of everything you can a sacrifice, and offer it to God as an act of reparation for the sins by which He is offended, and in supplication for the conversion of sinners"... "and say many times... 'O Jesus, it is for love of You, for the conversion of sinners, and in reparation for the sins committed against the Immaculate Heart of Mary.'"Thou has saved the best wine until now!

One Our Father, 10 Hail Marys, One Glory Be, Decade Prayer

Prayer

Grace of the mystery of Our Lord's first miracle, come down into my soul and make me faithful and generous..

The Proclamation of the Kingdom of God & the Call to Repentance

"Jesus Proclaims the Kingdom"

+Mark 1:14-15
Matthew 13:24-34 / Matthew 13:36-43
/ Matthew 13:44-52

Prayer

We offer Thee, O Lord Jesus, this decade in honor of the Proclamation of Thy Kingdom and the Call to Repentance, and we ask of Thee, through this mystery and through the intercession of Thy Blessed Mother, an awareness of God's Kingdom within us and to be truly repentant.

Scripture

"And after that John was delivered up, Jesus came into Galilee, preaching the gospel of the kingdom of God, and saying: 'The time is accomplished, and the kingdom of God is at hand: repent, and believe the gospel.'"

Meditation

Jesus spent three years proclaiming the Good News of the Kingdom. All were blessed to witness the tender, yet fierce love of Israel's God. In the Gospels we find not only the immensity of God's saving wisdom in Jesus' public ministry, but also the bewildering array of responses offered by fallen humanity; and in that story we find our own. May we never tire of drinking from the well of Jesus' teachings and reverencing the Gospels as the daily bread that alone can satisfy our soul's hunger for holiness.

Fatima Reflection

"What do you want of me?" Lucia's question at each apparition reveals an eagerness of heart that can be ours in seeking the Will of God. Our Lord instructs, *"Suffer the little children to come unto Me, for of such is the kingdom of Heaven."* Our Lady comes with a Message for childlike souls who wish to learn of the Kingdom of God. *"Are you willing to offer yourselves to God to bear all the sufferings He wills to send you...?"* The faithful fulfillment of duties God seeks and requires.

One Our Father, 10 Hail Marys, One Glory Be, Decade Prayer

Prayer

Grace of the mystery of the Proclamation of God's Kingdom and Call to Repentance, make me hunger and thirst for a deeper union with Christ present in my soul.

The Transfiguration
"Jesus Transfigured"
+Mark 9:1-8
Luke 9:28-36 / Matthew 17:1-9

Prayer

We offer Thee, O Lord Jesus, this decade in honor of Thy Transfiguration, and we ask of Thee, through this mystery and through the intercession of Thy Blessed Mother, spiritual courage.

Scripture

"... Jesus taketh with him Peter and James and John, and leadeth them up into a high mountain apart by themselves, and was transfigured before them... And there was a cloud overshadowing them: and a voice came out of the cloud, saying: 'This is my most beloved son; hear ye him.'"

Meditation

In this mystery of light, the Lord ascends Mount Tabor to manifest His glory to His inner circle of disciples. They witness Moses and Elijah conversing with the glorified Jesus of His upcoming Passion and discover the unity of the Old Testament's witness to Jesus' destiny, as well as the hope that awaits them on the far side of Golgotha. May we also find faith in the mysterious providence of God that penetrates life's darkest corners. *Per Crucem ad Lucem: "Through the Cross to the Light."*

Fatima Reflection

Our Lady, transfigured in Her heavenly state, opened Her hands and bathed the children in light which penetrated their souls, making them see themselves in God. They were caught up in the ecstasy of what participation in the life of God means: *"O most Holy Trinity, I adore You! My God, my God, I love You in the most Blessed Sacrament!"* This memory was to carry them through their trials, just as the Blessed Sacrament will be our strength during ours.

One Our Father, 10 Hail Marys, One Glory Be, Decade Prayer

Prayer

Grace of the mystery of the Transfiguration, come down into my soul and strengthen it in fortitude.

The Institution of the Holy Eucharist
"Jesus Gives Himself as Food"
+Luke 22:14-20
Mark 14:22-26 / Matthew 26:26-30

THE EUCHARIST

Prayer

We offer Thee, O Lord Jesus, this decade in honor of the Holy Eucharist, wherein Thou didst sacrificially give Thine own Body and Blood to be our Food, made possible through Mary's gift of self, and we ask of Thee, through this mystery and through the intercession of Thy most Holy Mother, a deep and intimate love for Thee in the Most Blessed Sacrament of the Altar.

Scripture

"And he said to them: ' With desire I have desired to eat this pasch with you before I suffer. For I say to you, that from this time I will not eat it, till it be fulfilled in the kingdom of God.'"

Meditation

In the institution of the Eucharist, the Lord Jesus left us a token of a love beyond all human comprehension. So great was His desire to grant us a total sharing in His Divine Life that He shattered the substance of bread and wine and filled them with Himself. It was the gift of His paschal sacrifice that He left mystically hidden in the Eucharist, that we who receive should become what we eat and drink: living sacrifices of love broken and offered for the life of the world. May the Lord, who offered this precious Gift, preserve us in faith, hope, and love, that we may never be parted from Him now or in the world to come.

Fatima Reflection

The Fatima Message is Christ-centered in the Heart of Mary. Our Lady leads us to be Eucharistic-centered by uniting our heart with Hers. Reparation is an expression of love which consoles the pain of the Beloved. *"Take and drink the Body and Blood of Jesus Christ, horribly outraged by ungrateful men! Make reparation for their crimes and console your God."* Offer it *"in reparation for the outrages, sacrileges, and indifference with which he is offended."* In showing mercy, we are shown mercy.

One Our Father, 10 Hail Marys, One Glory Be, Decade Prayer

Prayer

Grace of the mystery of the Institution of the Holy Eucharist, come down into my soul and inflame me with the fire of love for Christ truly present in the Most Blessed Sacrament.

The Agony in the Garden

"Jesus in His Agony
+Luke 22:39-46
Matthew 26:36-46 / Mark 14:32-42

Prayer

We offer Thee, O Lord Jesus, this decade in honor of Thy Mortal Agony in the Garden of Olives, and we ask of Thee, through this mystery and through the intercession of Thy Blessed Mother, perfect sorrow for our sins and the virtue of perfect obedience to Thy Holy Will.

Scripture

"... kneeling down, he prayed, saying, 'Father, if thou wilt, remove this chalice from me: but yet not my will, but thine be done.' And there appeared to him an angel from heaven, strengthening him. And being in an agony, he prayed the longer. And his sweat became as drops of blood, trickling down upon the ground."

Meditation

Jesus' participation in the anxieties of His agony lead us to consider how to act when it seems all our strength, supports, and even our friends, have left us in our time of need. It is in that moment we must face the knowledge of our Heavenly Father's Will, and our inner pain of natural resistance, to accept what we have no power to change. *"And being in an agony, He prayed the longer."*

Fatima Reflection

The children were trained in the exercise of prayer, as directed by the angel, to make sacrifices that were necessary to save souls, and as a means to overcome their own natural feelings of recoiling from difficulty. Falling prostrate, they would pray for hours offering to the Lord all that mortified them, repeating the prayer the angel taught them. Jesus said, *"The spirit is willing but the flesh is weak,"* yet, like Jesus, these children exercised their will in prayer to overcome temptation and weakness.

One Our Father, 10 Hail Marys, One Glory Be, Decade Prayer

Prayer

Grace of the mystery of Our Lord's Agony, come down into my soul and make me truly contrite and perfectly obedient to Thy Will.

The Scourging at the Pillar
"Jesus Scourged"
+Luke 23:13-25
Matthew 27:11-26 / Mark 15:1-15
/ John 18:37-40; 19:1

Prayer

We offer Thee, O Lord Jesus, this decade in honor of Thy Bloody Scourging, and we ask of Thee, through this mystery and through the intercession of Thy Blessed Mother, the grace to mortify our senses perfectly.

Scripture

"[Pilate] said to them: 'You have presented unto me this man, as one that perverteth the people; and behold I, having examined him before you, find no cause...in those things wherein you accuse him... I will chastise him therefore, and release him' ...but Jesus he delivered up to their will."

Meditation

Vehemently accused by the chief priests, Jesus did not return accusations or justify Himself before Pilate. And in a man-made hour of mercy, a man of death is chosen to be freed of his prison, while Christ our Life is delivered to death - He Who so desires to free us from the prison we create by what we choose to do of our own free will. How forcefully do we impose our will in our dealings with others? How easily do we back down before the insistent force of those who have no respect for the least among us?

Fatima Reflection

The shepherd children, from very early on, had to overcome human respect and the scourging of words: the incessant attention, the false accusations, even threats of death. They held fast to their appointed task, and to the truth, for in Mary they heard His voice. We must all have the determination of martyrs, in the face of every obstacle, to hold firm to the fullness of our Catholic Faith to the end.

One Our Father, 10 Hail Marys, One Glory Be, Decade Prayer

Prayer

Grace of Our Lord's Scourging, come down into my soul and make me truly mortified.

The Crowning with Thorns
"Jesus Crowned with Thorns"
+ John 19:2-16
Matthew 27:27-31 / Mark 15:16-20

Prayer

We offer Thee, O Lord Jesus, this decade in honor of Thy Cruel Crowning with Thorns, and we ask of Thee, through this mystery and through the intercession of Thy Blessed Mother, a great contempt of the world.

Scripture

"And the soldiers platting a crown of thorns, put it upon his head; and they put on him a purple garment. And they came to him, and said: 'Hail, king of the Jews'; and they gave him blows... [Pilate] saith to them: 'Behold the Man... Shall I crucify your king?' The chief priests answered: 'We have no king but Caesar.' Then therefore he [Pilate] delivered him to them to be crucified."

Meditation

Christ is ridiculed as a mock king. They hailed Him as "the Son of David Who comes in the Name of the Lord" upon His entry into the Holy City; yet shortly thereafter, they said, "We have no king but Caesar!" The only earthly crown Jesus accepts is the crown of thorns. What could possibly be a reason for such a radical rejection of Jesus and of His Kingdom? The terms of accepting Christ's Kingship exclude determining for ourselves the law by which we are to live.

Fatima Reflection

In the humble ways of a child, which Jesus bids us to live, the Fatima children submit to the demands of their parents, Church leaders and government officials. Yet in all of its agonizing circumstances, the children kept their priorities straight. There is no power except that which is given from above. Jesus does not use His Power to assert His personal rights; and the Fatima children surrender themselves to God's Power, Who prevails in the end.

One Our Father, 10 Hail Marys, One Glory Be, Decade Prayer

Prayer

Grace of the mystery of Our Lord's Crowning with Thorns, come down into my soul and make me despise the world.

39

Jesus Carries the Cross

"Jesus Carrying His Cross"
+Luke 23:26-32
Matthew 27:32-33 / Mark 15:21-22

Prayer

We offer Thee, O Lord Jesus, this decade in honor of Thy Carrying Thy Cross and we ask of Thee, through this mystery and through the intercession of Thy Blessed Mother, to give us great patience in carrying our cross in Thy footsteps every day of our life.

Scripture

"And as they led him away...they laid the cross on [Simon of Cyrene] to carry after Jesus...Women...bewailed and lamented him... 'Weep not over me; but weep for yourselves, and for your children. For behold, the days shall come, wherein they will say: Blessed are the barren...Then shall they begin to say to the mountains: Fall upon us; ...Cover us. For if in the green wood they do these things, what shall be done in the dry?'"

Meditation

Jesus, as if to bear up the lives of each of us as a family upon His shoulders, takes up His Cross. Without Jesus looking to seek relief, they laid hold of Simon; though not for the sake of charity. Women lament Him, but Jesus directs their grief to the source of His affliction – the rejection of His Life and Love; like sinful lifeless wombs through contraception and abortion in our day. (Luke 23:29-31, Is. 2:19, Rev. 6:16-17)

Fatima Reflection

"Penance! Penance! Penance!" was the cry of the avenging angel of the Third Secret whose fiery sword was prevented by Our Lady from striking the earth. *"Pray, pray very much, and make sacrifices for sinners,"* Our Lady pleads, *"for many souls go to hell because there are none to sacrifice themselves and to pray for them."* In imitation of the loving Hearts of Jesus and Mary, let us direct all things to glorify God, and to save souls, to keep the waters of grace flowing.

One Our Father, 10 Hail Marys, One Glory Be, Decade Prayer

Prayer

Grace of the mystery of the Carrying of the Cross, come down into my soul and make me truly patient.

The Crucifixion
"Jesus Crucified"
+John 19:17-30
Matthew 27:33-50 / Mark 15:22-37 / Luke 19:17-30 /
Luke 23:33-47

Prayer

We offer Thee, O Lord Jesus, this decade in honor of Thy Crucifixion on Mt. Calvary, and we ask of Thee, through this mystery and through the intercession of Thy Blessed Mother, a great horror of sin, a love of the Cross, and the grace of a holy death for us and for those who are now in their last agony.

Scripture

"...he went forth to that place which is called Calvary...where they crucified him...Now there stood by the cross of Jesus, his mother, ...and the disciple standing whom he loved... 'Woman, behold thy son'...to the disciple: 'Behold thy mother.' ...when he had taken the vinegar... bowing his head, he gave up the ghost."

Meditation

Jesus experienced utter desolation, refusing to deliver Himself from death. Who overcomes when even faith is at the brink of being lost? The answer is found where the heart is formed: *"Woman, behold thy son."* After that He said to the disciple: *"Behold thy Mother."*

Fatima Reflection

What could motivate children to want to give up their lunch, or refuse to drink water in the heat of summer, or choose to wear stiff bristled ropes day and night, or to suffer still more when a choice is given to go on suffering or receive now the promise of heaven? Today, children and adults alike, are unwilling to give up anything that pleases themselves. It is only through devotion to Mary that we can take refuge in Her Immaculate Heart and find therein the way that leads us to God.

One Our Father, 10 Hail Marys, One Glory Be, Decade Prayer

Prayer

Grace of the mystery of the Death and Passion of Our Lord and Savior Jesus Christ, come down into my soul and make me truly holy.

The Resurrection
"Jesus Risen from the Dead"
+Luke 24:36-48
Matthew 28:1-15 / Mark 16:1-14 / Luke 24:1-12 /
Luke 24:13-35/John 20:1-10 / John 20:11-18 /
John 20:19-29 / John 21:1-14

Prayer
We offer Thee, O Lord Jesus, this decade in honor of Thy Triumphant Resurrection, and we ask of Thee, through this mystery and through the intercession of Thy Blessed Mother, a lively faith.

Scripture

"And he said to them: 'Thus it is written, and thus it behooved Christ to suffer, and to rise again from the dead, the third day: and that penance and remission of sins should be preached in his name, unto all nations... you are witnesses of these things.'"

Meditation

Jesus, having conquered death with life, and sin with love, appears to the women and His followers, at various times and in various ways, to deliver a pro-life message that goes beyond what this finite existence is able to contain. Christ's power is over life and death in this world and in the next! LOVE is more powerful than death; LIFE reaches beyond the grave for those who believe. Suffering has saving power! Penance, and remission of sins in Christ, saves souls.

Fatima Reflection

The day of the miracle had arrived. Not since the resurrection was a miracle of this magnitude ever foretold. Undaunted by the fears of those who said it might not take place, Lucia believed; and her faith was not disappointed. Our Lady keeps Her promises. The sun displayed its power, pilgrims cried out for mercy, some confessed their sins, conversions took place. Let us enter into partnership with Mary and faithfully keep our commitments for true peace. God cannot be outdone in generosity.

One Our Father, 10 Hail Marys, One Glory Be, Decade Prayer

Prayer

Grace of the mystery of the Resurrection, come down into my soul and make me truly faithful.

The Ascension
"Jesus Ascending to Heaven"
+Acts 1:4-12
Matthew 28:18-20 / Mark 16:15-20 /
Luke 24:46-53

Prayer

We offer Thee, O Lord Jesus, this decade in honor of Thy Glorious Ascension, and we ask of Thee, through this mystery and through the intercession of Thy Blessed Mother, a firm hope and a great longing for Heaven.

Scripture

"...you shall be witnesses unto me in Jerusalem, and in all Judea, and Samaria, and even to the uttermost part of the earth. And when he had said these things...he was raised up: and a cloud received him out of their sight."

Meditation

All that Jesus said and did, His Life He gave, His Spirit He imparted, was entrusted to His apostles, that they might preach to all nations, giving what they had received. As members of His Body, we, too, have a part in this commission to live out in our own lives what we have received from Christ in body and in spirit. His ascension into heaven is the incense of our presence in Christ before the Father, Who presents all our love and needs to Him, until God's Plan is fulfilled in making Jesus and Mary known and loved.

Fatima Reflection

Our Lady drew all three children to live a way of life that brought them to the heights of holiness in a very short period of time. Jacinta and Francisco were taken to heaven soon. But Lucia was to stay here some time longer. Do we recognize in this invitation the same call for us to spread the Gospel in our own day? *"Jesus wishes to make use of you to make Me known and loved. He wants to establish in the world devotion to My Immaculate Heart."* How will I respond?

One Our Father, 10 Hail Marys, One Glory Be, Decade Prayer

Prayer

Grace of the mystery of the Ascension of Our Lord, come down into my soul and make me ready for Heaven.

The Descent of the Holy Spirit
"Jesus Filling Thee with the Holy Spirit"
+Acts 2:1-18, 34-41

Prayer

We offer Thee, O Holy Spirit, this decade in honor of Pentecost, and we ask of Thee, through this mystery and through the intercession of Mary, Thy most faithful Spouse, Thy Holy Wisdom so that we may know, really love and practice Thy truth, and make all others share in it.

Scripture

"And they were all filled with the Holy Ghost, and they began to speak with diverse tongues...Now when [the multitude] had heard these things, they had compunction in their heart... But Peter said to them: Do penance, and be baptized...in the name of Jesus Christ, for the remission of your sins: and you shall receive the gift of the Holy Ghost."

Meditation

Compunction of the heart, penance, remission of sins: These are the work of the Holy Spirit, Who helps us choose to live without sin, like Mary *"... and they that work by me, shall not sin."* (Eccli. 24:30) As we come to realize our spiritual birth as members of the Church, let us live a new life for God as children of the Hearts of Jesus and Mary.

Fatima Reflection

"Offer prayers and sacrifices constantly to the Most High." Mary, Spouse of the Holy Spirit, can make supple our heart to receive all the inspirations God wishes to send us. When we deny ourselves, we can be moved by inspiration. Jesus can use us to bring light to a world in darkness which is moved only by its lusts and self interests. Let sacrificial love be the moving force of your life as the Fatima children allowed themselves to be moved, no longer acting according to their feelings and personal desires.

One Our Father, 10 Hail Marys, One Glory Be, Decade Prayer

Prayer

Grace of the mystery of Pentecost, come down into my soul and make me truly wise in the eyes of the Almighty God.

Our Lady's Assumption

"Jesus Raising Thee up Body and Soul into Heaven"
+ Ecclesiasticus 24:22-32
Ecclesiasticus 24:1-11 / Ecclesiasticus 24:12-19

Prayer

We offer Thee, O Lord Jesus, this decade in honor of the the Immaculate Conception and the Assumption of Thy Holy and Blessed Mother, Body and Soul into Heaven, and we ask of Thee, through these two mysteries and through Her intercession, the gift of true devotion to Her to help us live and die in holiness.

Scripture

"I am the mother of fair love, and of fear, and of knowledge, and of holy hope. In me is all grace of the way and of the truth, in me is all hope of life and of virtue. Come over to me, all ye that desire me, and be filled with my fruits...He that hearkeneth to me, shall not be confounded...They that explain me shall have life everlasting."

Meditation

"Then the Creator of all things commanded, and said to me: and He that made me, rested in my tabernacle" (Eccli. 24:12). All that can be said of Mary can be expressed in saying that She is all that any of us want to be in loving Jesus with the fullness of that love, which He deserves. She is the perfection of all the love He desires from us. We can offer our hearts to Him, united to Hers, offering a total love, which makes up for our deficiencies. Our Lady's assumption into heaven is `the incense of our presence in Mary's Immaculate Heart before Christ, who presents all of our love and needs to Him, to help us be disposed to fulfill God's Plan.

Fatima Reflection

Our Lady made known Her desire to have the Rosary recited every day. At the last apparition She held out the Brown Scapular because She wants us to wear it. Our Lady was not communicating a mere symbolic presence. She has given us a means to enter into a mystical union with Her, a union which is caught up in the mystery of Mary's bodily assumption. What does this suggest to you in your offering of prayers at Holy Communion?

One Our Father, 10 Hail Marys, One Glory Be, Decade Prayer

Prayer

Grace of the mysteries of the Immaculate Conception and the Assumption of Mary, come down into my soul and make me truly devoted to Her.

The Coronation of Our Lady as Queen of
Heaven and Earth
"Jesus Crowning Thee"
+Psalm 44:10-18
Revelation 12:1-8,13-17

Prayer

We offer Thee, O Lord Jesus, this decade in honor
of the Glorious Crowning of Thy Blessed Mother in
Heaven, and we ask of Thee, through this mystery
and through Her intercession, the grace of persever-
ance and increase of virtue until the very moment of
death and after that the eternal crown that is prepared
for us. We ask the same grace for all the just and for
all our benefactors.

Scripture

"On your right stands the queen in gold of Ophir... So will the king desire your beauty: he is your lord, pay homage to him...The daughter of the king is clothed with splendor, her robes embroidered with pearls set in gold. She is led to the king with her maiden companions...May the peoples praise you from age to age." [Office of Readings]

Meditation

As the world, lost through Adam, was restored through Christ, so also man sinned by the influence of a woman, and by a Woman, the old influence was replaced. Ave reverses Eva, and Live reverses Evil. By means of Mary, Christ crushes the head of Satan; and in the original translation of Gen. 3:15 ("She shall crush thy head"), we see Mary's role in playing Her part in God's Plan of salvation. As members of His Body, Jesus gathers us together in Himself, with Mary as Type and Model. In Her let us allow Christ to use us, too, in fulfilling our part in accomplishing His ultimate victory.

Fatima Reflection

"Continue to pray the Rosary everyday in honor of Our Lady of the Rosary, in order to obtain peace for the world and the end of the war; because only She can help you." Our Lady's role as Mother and Queen is intrinsic in our relationship with God, if we are to live according to God's pleasure. Not according to our ways does God see things, but according to His own. Therefore, let us fulfill the desire of Our Lord's Most Sacred Heart: to console Him by relieving the wounds directed against our Mother and Queen by means of the reparation of the Five First Saturdays for the conversion of sinners and for peace.

One Our Father, 10 Hail Marys, One Glory Be, Decade Prayer

Prayer

Grace of the mystery of the Coronation of the Blessed Mother in Heaven, convert sinners, help the dying, deliver the Holy Souls from purgatory and give us all Thy grace so that we may live and die well - and please give us the Light of Thy glory later on so that we may see Thee Face to face and love Thee for all eternity. Amen. So be it.

HAIL HOLY QUEEN:

Hail, Holy Queen, Mother of Mercy, our life, our sweetness and our hope. To Thee do we cry, poor banished children of Eve. To Thee do we send up our sighs, mourning and weeping in this valley of tears.

Turn then, most gracious Advocate, Thine eyes of mercy towards us; and after this, our exile, show unto us the Blessed Fruit of Thy womb, Jesus. O clement, O loving, O sweet Virgin Mary!

V. Pray for us, Queen of the most Holy Rosary.

R. That we may be made worthy of the promises of Christ.

LET US PRAY:

Oh God, Whose only begotten Son, by his life, death and resurrection, has purchased for us the rewards of eternal life; grant we beseech Thee, that meditating on these Mysteries of the most Holy Rosary of the Blessed Virgin Mary, we may imitate what they contain, and obtain what they promise, through the same Christ, Our Lord. *Amen.*

ST. MICHAEL PRAYER

St. Michael, the Archangel, defend us in battle. Be our protection against the wickedness and the snares of the devil. May God rebuke him, we humbly pray, and do thou, O Prince of the heavenly hosts, by the power of God, cast into hell Satan and all the evil spirits, who prowl about the world seeking the ruin of souls. *Amen.*

PRAYER FOR THE HOLY FATHER AND HIS INTENTIONS:

May be used in place of one Our Father, Hail Mary, and Glory Be.

O Lord, Source of Eternal Life and Truth, give to Your Shepherd, [Current Pope's Name], a spirit of courage and right judgment, a spirit of knowledge and love. By governing with fidelity those entrusted to his care, may he as successor of the Apostle Peter and Vicar of Christ, build Your Church into a sacrament of unity, love and peace for all the world. We ask this through Our Lord Jesus Christ, Your Son, Who lives and reigns with You and the Holy Spirit, one God forever and ever. *Amen*

MARY, MOTHER FOR LIFE:

O Mary, Mother of the Life Within, all life we entrust to You: the life of every expectant mother and the child within her womb, the life of every human body, the life of every human soul, the life of every newborn child and the life of all grown old. You held the Lord to Your own Heart and drew Him so close in. So draw us now in all our needs, O Mother of the Life Within.

INVOCATION OF FATIMA PATRONS:

Most Sacred Heart of Jesus, **Have mercy on us!**

Sorrowful and Immaculate Heart of Mary, **Pray for us!**

Our Lady of the Rosary, **Pray for us!**

Our Lady of Fatima, **Pray for us!**

St. Joseph, **Pray for us!**

St. Pio of Pietrelcina, **Pray for us!**

St. Louis de Montfort, **Pray for us!**

St. Maximilian Kolbe, **Pray for us!**

St. Dominic and St. Simon Stock, **Pray for us!**

St. Therese of the Child Jesus, **Pray for us!**

St. Anthony Mary Claret, **Pray for us!**

Blessed Jacinta and Blessed Francisco, **Pray for us!**

[Saint of the Day], **Pray for us!**

All you holy angels and saints, **Pray for us!**

V. May the Divine Assistance remain with us always.

R. And may the souls of the faithful departed, through the mercy of God, rest in peace. *Amen.*

Please Stand

FATIMA AVE:

Refrain: Ave, Ave, Ave Maria.
                Ave, Ave, Ave Maria.

                Our thanks to the Godhead
                Whose ways are so sure
                For giving us Mary
                Our Mother most pure.

                                      Refrain

Prayer Cell Formation Program

FORMATION PROGRAM:
Available free. Download at www.wafusa.org
The Formation Program is a step-by-step study guide that
includes a 4 level growth process. All 4 levels include:

- Spiritual Reading
- Reflection and Resolution
- Silent Reflection
- Discussion
- Examination by Cell Members
- Apostolic Resolution
- Act of Consecration

Step I forms one in the spirituality of the Message of
Fatima through a more in depth look into the words of
Lucia Speaks. Once this first level completes its first
year, it splits to form a new Prayer Cell moving to Step
II using the same process. All levels are on-going to
allow for new members to join at any time, attend les-
sons they missed, or repeat a level before moving on
to the next step.

+ Come, Holy Spirit, fill the hearts of Thy faithful and enkindle in them the fire of Thy love.

V. Send forth Thy Spirit and they shall be created.

R. And Thou shalt renew the face of the earth.

LET US PRAY. O God, Who didst instruct the hearts of the faithful by the light of the Holy Spirit, grant us, in the same Spirit, to be truly wise and ever to rejoice in His consolation, through Christ Our Lord. *Amen.*

SPIRITUAL READING:

Read from one of the spiritual books listed below or listen to a talk given by the Spiritual Director or Cell Leader.

■ **Prayer Cell Formation Program -**
Step I: LUCIA SPEAKS
The Message of Fatima,
one apparition per month
Step II: THE TEN COMMANDMENTS
Section Two of Part Three in the
Catechism of the Catholic Church
Step III: "CALLS" FROM THE
MESSAGE OF FATIMA
By Sister Lucia dos Santos
Step IV: ANY APPROVED
FATIMA MATERIAL
Choose from the following,
or other approved resources:

- Fatima in Lucia's Own Words
- There is Nothing More
- Articles from SOUL Magazine
- The Holy Bible passages
- True Devotion to Mary, Secret of the Rosary, or other books by St. Louis de Montfort
- Aim Higher by St. Maximilian Kolbe
- Imitation of Christ by Thomas a'Kempis
- Encyclicals and writings by the Pope
- Books on Marian Spirituality
- Books by or about Fatima Patrons
- Any World Apostolate of Fatima publication

REFLECTION AND RESOLUTION:
Silently reflect on the readings or talk and after some discussion, determine resolution privately, as a group, or as presented in the lesson. Decide how to help others live, learn and spread our Lady of Fatima's message of hope for a world in great need.

EXAMINATION BY CELL MEMBERS:
Ask questions like: "How well did we keep our personal and apostolic resolutions?" or "What have we done to further the Message of Fatima?"

ACT OF CONSECRATION:

IMMACULATE HEART OF MARY, Queen of heaven and earth and tender Mother of men, in accordance with Thy ardent wish made known at Fatima, I consecrate to Thee myself, my brethren, my country and the whole human race. Reign over us and teach us how to make the Heart of Jesus reign and triumph in us and around us as It has reigned and triumphed in Thee.

Reign over us, dearest Mother, that we may be Thine in prosperity and in adversity, in joy and in sorrow, in health and in sickness, in life and in death. O most compassionate Heart of Mary, Queen of Virgins, watch over our minds and hearts and preserve them from the deluge of impurity which Thou didst lament so sorrowfully at Fatima. We want to be pure like Thee. We want to atone for the many sins committed against Jesus and Thee. We want to call down upon our country and the whole world the peace of God in justice and charity.

Therefore, we now promise to imitate Thy virtues by the practice of a Christian life without regard to human respect. We resolve to receive Holy Communion on the first Saturday of every month and to offer Thee five decades of the Rosary each day together with our sacrifices in a spirit of reparation and penance. *Amen.*